£6.⁰⁰

CW01033066

THE NORTH EAST
RAILWAY BOOK

Ken Hoole

David & Charles

Newton Abbot London North Pomfret (Vt)

British Library Cataloguing in Publication Data
Hoole, Kenneth
  The North East Railway
  1. Railroads — England — History
  I. Title
  385'.09428   HE3019.N/
  ISBN 0 7153 7683 7

Set and printed in Great Britain by Biddles Limited
Guildford, for David & Charles (Publishers) Limited
Brunel House Newton Abbot Devon

Published in the United States of America
by David & Charles Inc
North Pomfret Vermont 05053 USA

CONTENTS

PREFACE

The North Eastern Railway has long been neglected. Over the years I have tried to reverse the position and to obtain for the North Eastern the recognition it deserves as one of Britain's most progressive and efficient railways. Certainly it had a virtual monopoly, but only on rare occasions did it use its monopolistic powers, and then only when it considered it was for the general good.

The period from 1923 to 1947, during which time it became the North Eastern Area of the LNER, was a time of comparatively little change considering the difficulties through which the country was passing, but since the formation of British Railways on 1 January 1948 the old North Eastern system has been decimated by 30 years of withdrawals and closures.

This work, therefore, is to honour the North Eastern and its successors, and also the countless thousands of staff who have served the railways of North Eastern England for almost two centuries.

K. HOOLE

(Illustrations not credited are from the author's collection or taken by the author.)

INTRODUCTION

Improvements in the use of steam power in the last quarter of the eighteenth century paved the way for the development of the steam locomotive in the first quarter of the nineteenth century. It it not certain who actually invented the steam locomotive, although Richard Trevithick has a very strong claim to that distinction, but once it was proved that steam could be used to power an 'Iron Horse' development was rapid, especially in areas where minerals were worked. This was because cheaper and improved methods of transport were always being sought, particularly in mining areas where it was necessary to get coal from the mine to the consumer as economically as possible. Consequently in Northumberland and Durham, on opposite banks of the River Tyne, various men were striving to construct practical steam locomotives suitable for hauling wagons of coal from the pithead to the shipping points (staiths) on the banks of the river. Among them were William Hedley and George Stephenson, the latter founding in 1823 the firm of Robert Stephenson & Co to specialise in the building of locomotives; he was also responsible for planning and supervising the construction of the Hetton Railway, opened in 1822, and the Stockton & Darlington Railway, opened in 1825, the world's first steam worked public railway.

Because of its location on the line of the Stockton & Darlington Railway (which did not actually terminate at Darlington but at Witton Park, some distance to the north west) Darlington became an important locomotive building centre and the products of William & Alfred Kitching, John Harris, I'Anson & Co, Robert Stephenson & Co, and the NER's North Road Engine Works are illustrated in this work. The North east was also notable for the number of concerns which built locomotives for their own use, for example Albert Hill Ironworks, Darlington, the Earl of Durham's Railway, Philadelphia, near Sunderland, and the Londonderry Railway at Seaham Harbour; there were also numerous small engine building concerns scattered throughout County Durham which turned their hand to locomotive construction when the demand was large and the results profitable.

The large number of steam locomotives at work at the many collieries, quarries, shipyards and chemical works, also brought a demand for firms which specialised in the repair of locomotives; some, moreover, also acted as dealers, rebuilding and reconditioning locomotives they had bought for resale. Well known names in this field were J.F. Wake of Darlington, T.D. Ridley (later Ridley, Shaw & Co Ltd) of Middlesbrough, and Lingford, Gardiner of Bishop Auckland. This led to the introduction of some strange types to the North east as these dealers purchased bargains in Southern England, or South Wales, and resold them to industrialists in Durham and Northumberland. Thus it was possible to see engines from the London, Brighton & South Coast, Taff Vale, Barry and Great Eastern railways, and many others besides, hard at work in the North East.

Some of the colliery systems had large fleets of locomotives and one, the Lambton, Hetton & Joicey combine, had more than 50, with its own works where extensive overhauls and rebuildings were carried out. The largest locomotive

Commemorative stone on the wall of the George & Dragon Hotel, Yarm.

A platelayers' hut at Simpasture Junction in 1925, where the Clarence Railway of 1833 joined the Stockton & Darlington Railway of 1825; it is probable that this was originally a shelter for the pointsman controlling the junction. The Clarence Railway could reach the pits in the Shildon area only by running over part of the Stockton & Darlington system, a practice which the Stockton & Darlington did not favour as it meant that such traffic was being abstracted from its own line!

works in the area however was the North Road Engine Works in Darlington, opened by the Stockton & Darlington Railway in 1863 and taken over by the North Eastern Railway later the same year. The NER also had works at Gateshead but it was closed in 1932 and the work transferred to Darlington, which became responsible for the overhaul of all the engines in the North Eastern Area, plus others from the former Great Northern, Great Central, Great Eastern and North British railways.

Over the years far too little attention has been paid to the countless men — and women — who have served the railways in their long existence. Not only were there the station staff and train crews with which the travelling public came into daily contact, but many other grades employing their skills and experience behind the scenes to keep the system working smoothly and safely.

People think of the driver as the man who guided their train safely from A to B, but what about the signalmen who carefully passed it on

its way, and the permanent way staff who, in all weathers, maintained the track to a high standard? And what about the bridge inspectors, surveying every bridge over or under the line, or the men with the particularly cold and filthy job of inspecting the interior of every dark, dank and dirty tunnel?

The steam locomotive itself, for long the centre of attention, required frequent maintenance, filling the tender with coal and water, cleaning the char out of the smokebox and the clinker from the firebox. The shed staff had all this to do. The working parts of a steam locomotive moreover were heavy and cumbersome, and far too often were in awkward positions which were difficult to reach. Unfortunately in this country there was far too little co-operation between the staff responsible for designing and building locomotives and those who worked on them or drove them in everyday service.

You may have had the rare privilege of standing on the footplate of a steam locomotive when it was stationary and, perhaps, on a cold and frosty morning, taken advantage of a warm from the firebox, but how different it is when an engine is on the move. A steel wheel on a steel rail does not give a smooth and quiet ride when up to 100 tons of engine is moving on the rails. As soon as the driver opened the regulator there was that fascinating sound of the steam rushing through the valve to the cylinders, then the sound of the first exhaust

beat and the first flicker of the fire. As the engine began to move, the bangs, creaks and rattles increased, particularly if the wheels at first failed to grip and spun freely, but even when running smoothly on straight track there was enough noise to make conversation difficult.

Another point that always struck me when I was privileged to ride on the footplate was the change that came over the crew as the engine began laboriously to get its heavy train on the move; they may have been fiercely discussing a certain horse-race, the merits of the local brew, or even politics, but, once they were moving, all their concentration was on the signals and the behaviour of the engine. Conversation was limited to brief reports and acknowledgement of whether signals ahead were 'on' or 'off', and sometimes even these details were conveyed across the cab by hand-signals. Every few minutes the fireman would open the firehole door and put a fairly precise number of shovelsful of coal on the fire, carefully placed round the grate to ensure even burning, but he would invariably cease firing at the opportune moment to catch sight of a signal which could first be seen from his side of the cab, perhaps one that was round a curve or over some trees. With their long experience every driver, and most firemen, knew exactly the point from which each signal could be seen, and most drivers were only too pleased to pass on their knowledge to their fireman, who had hopes of

Weigh cabin near Whitby about 1900. This was built by the Whitby & Pickering Railway, of which the eastern section was opened in 1835. Both British Rail and the local authority have declined to maintain this historic building and it is now little more than a heap of stone blocks.

becoming a driver himself one day. If a driver and fireman did not get on well together it was best that they were separated as soon as possible. The footplate of an express travelling at speed was no place to have petty arguments.

The days of one crew to one engine, or two crews to one engine, have long since gone, although at some of the smaller depots this practice continued almost until the end of steam traction. With their own engine the crews looked after it much better than an engine they handled for half a turn of duty, and then did not see again for days, weeks, or even months. One writer recalled years ago seeing the driver af a North Eastern Class Z Atlantic hauling a Newcastle-Liverpool express, get down from his cab during the stop at Ripon to wipe over the polished front buffers of his engine. It had started to rain and he carefully greased the buffer heads before starting away for the next stop at Harrogate.

Drivers and firemen were proud of their engines and liked to be photographed on or alongside them. Fortunately a number of such photographs have survived, often in the possession of children and grandchildren, who

7

can vaguely remember the old man in his blue dungarees, and also the unusual hours he used to keep, for railways are a 24 hour service and crews are required at all times of day and night to work both passenger and freight trains.

Signalmen had their contrasting conditions; in a small cabin on a branch line there was often no one to talk to, whereas in a large and busy cabin, with two, three, or four men on duty at a time, there was no opportunity for idle chatter. Full concentration was needed and the only conversation was about traffic and shunting movements, interrupted frequently by the jangling of the telephone bells as other boxes and control reported deviations from the timetable and the steps to be taken to work the traffic as expeditiously as possible. Almost to a man signalmen were — and still are — a conscientious body of men; they had to be to carry out their duties when many lives depended upon strict adherence to the rules. Rules were designed to prevent accidents on railways, and they usually succeeded; when trouble arose it was usually because two or more men ignored the rules at the same time, thus losing the intended safeguard of one man's actions being a check on the other. This is brought out frequently in the fascinating accident reports, issued for well over a century by government appointed inspectors, whether at various times from the Board of Trade, the Ministry of Transport, or the Department of the Environment.

Permanent way staff were usually seen leaning on their shovels as a train passed, but what else could they do? Far too many men have lost their lives while working on the track, and in this day of trains travelling at up to 125mph their task is even more potentially dangerous. Now, however, far more track work is being carried out by on-track machines, and this often requires regular trains to be diverted (usually at week-ends), when lines are blocked by maintenance machines.

In the days of semaphore signals using oil lamps the permanent way men were called out at all hours to go 'fogging', standing at a signal with flags, lamps and detonators; sometimes he had a glowing brazier to keep him warm in the cold fog and swirling steam, and essential refreshment was provided at the railways expense if he was on duty for sufficient hours! The permanent way men also had the dirty end of the stick if there was a heavy snowfall; they had first to clear the points and rodding, signals and wires, and then, if there was a complete blockage, dig the snow away to free a trapped train. The trans Pennine lines of the NER often suffered in a severe winter.

Contractors opening out Richmond Hill tunnel, Leeds, in the 1890s. The original tunnel, built by the Leeds & Selby Railway, opened in 1834, was converted to a wide and deep cutting which is still in use.

Locomotives had to be overhauled regularly at the main workshops; day to day repairs and adjustments were carried out at running sheds, but when the boiler had to be removed, new cylinders were required, or any task beyond the capabilities of the shed, then the engine had to go to 'works'. In the nineteenth century the North Eastern Railway had works at a number of the larger railway towns, but by the turn of the century only those at York, Gateshead and Darlington remained in use. York closed in 1905 and Gateshead in 1932, leaving only North Road Works at Darlington to maintain all the engines in the North Eastern Area of the LNER.

For more than a century they carried out extensive repairs and renewals, supplying new frames, fireboxes, boilers and cylinders, turning out engines in a coat of new paint, green for all engines until 1904, then green for the passenger engines and black for the goods engines, an economy measure estimated to save £7,000 a year! A reduction in the number of LNER classes to be painted green, introduced in 1928 as a further economy measure,

Completing the Whitby, Redcar & Middlesbrough Union Railway in the 1880s, with the south end of Grinkle tunnel in the background. The line was closed in 1958 but was subsequently relaid and reopened for mineral traffic from a new potash mine at Boulby, near Staithes.

brought about the dismissal of nine painters and the reduction in grade of seven others! Railway employment, although fairly regular, was not a sinecure and men were dismissed, laid off, or put on short time, depending on the state of the traffic. In the slump of the early 1930s many footplate staff were redundant and firemen were downgraded to cleaners, while cleaners were often glad to take jobs as porters. As trade and traffic improved they were recalled to the locomotive department and many retired as drivers in the 1960s.

The North Eastern Railway was notable for the statistics it compiled to show up inefficiencies in its system, and in 1902 a traffic statistics office was set up in York under C.P. Mossop, who later became Assistant to the General Manager. The company issued an invaluable series of booklets to its officers, such as traffic statistics, mineral statistics, population tables and passenger bookings, expenses at junctions with other companies, and locomotive statistics. Thus at a glance one could see the amount of each type of traffic conveyed, the revenue it brought in, and the cost of working it. Taking the last full year before World War I, for instance, the NER carried 43,030,426 tons of mineral traffic in the year, or approximately 140,000 tons every working day. Another interesting item is that North Eastern locomotives consumed 976,326 tons of coal in 1913, or 7.19% of the national

consumption by locomotives.

Coal was shipped for export at numerous ports and harbours along the North East coast from Hull to Tweedmouth and those handling the largest quantities were:

	Tons		Tons
Tyne Dock	7,139,651	Lambton Staiths	1,918,277*
Hull	3,590,299	East Hartlepool	1,829,463
North Blyth	2,866,669	South Blyth	1,420,011
Dunston	2,776,380	Sunderland	1,352,043

*this traffic was conveyed over the NER from Penshaw but shipped at the colliery company's staiths.
(Incidentally the NER always used staiths, never staithes. The latter was the name of a station near Whitby!)

The coal output of the United Kingdom in 1913 was 287,430,473 tons, of which Northumberland produced 14,819,284 tons, and County Durham 41,532,890 tons. Coal and coke carried in 1913 by the railways serving the principal coal mining areas amounted to:

	Tons
North Eastern	44,165,950
Midland	27,834,531
London & North Western	23,496,970

North Eastern locomotives worked regularly to Edinburgh on East Coast expresses and this is the pioneer engine of Fletcher's famous 901 class standing at Waverley station. The Rainbow dining rooms in the background disappeared with the construction of the new North Bridge and the remodelling of the station in the 1890s. The driver is Enoch Shipley (later a locomotive inspector) who was driving 901 when it was derailed at Morpeth in 1877.

	Tons
Great Western	22,142,823
North British	21,233,792
Taff Vale	15,682,640
Caledonian	13,026,909

In County Durham large quantities of coke were produced for iron and steel making, and not only for ironworks in the North East, for large amounts were supplied to West Cumberland. The 1913 statistics show:

Coal used to make coke in	
County Durham	9,153,636 tons
Coke produced from above	5,822,799 tons

The coke came from 9,578 ovens, of which 7,326 were of the 'beehive' type, which were being replaced by larger and more modern designs of ovens. The number of 'beehive' ovens in 1905 was 14,259!

North Eastern engines did not work regularly to Kings Cross, but in the 1920s and 1930s they could often be seen in London on excursions, especially on cup final days if a North east team (or teams) was involved. This is Class C7 No 2168, one of the famous NER class Z Atlantics, standing at Kings Cross shed awaiting its return working to York, Darlington and Teesside.

The Carnforth, Furness and West Cumberland traffic amounted to:

via Tebay	via Redhills Curve (Penrith)	via Carlisle	Total
		Tons	Tons
528,942	116,482	389,079	1,034,503

The blast furnaces in the North East also required large quantities of ironstone and iron ore, and, until imported ore gained a hold, the mineral was mined locally in Cleveland, where the NER carried 6,039,659 tons in 1913. In the same period the Durham ore carried amounted to 36 tons!

In addition to a fleet of 65,796 miscellaneous goods wagons the North Eastern had an almost equally large fleet of mineral wagons totalling 58,743. Examples of the more common types were:

8 — 12 ton capacity	32,570
15 — 17 ton capacity	1,783
20 ton capacity	17,455
40 ton capacity	100
West Cumberland coke 10½ ton capacity	533
Coke 8 & 10 ton capacity	2,978
Convertible 10½ ton	471
Ironstone 8 & 10½ ton capacity	51
Ironstone 20 & 30 ton capacity	738

The number of chaldron wagons was falling rapidly at this time and 1913 was the first year when a nil return was quoted. In 1912 they had been reduced to 34, from 510 in 1907.

The North Eastern, like many other railways, ran its own fire brigades at such centres as Hull, York, Darlington, Newcastle etc. For many years they were provided with horse-drawn steam fire engines, which could be loaded on to railway wagons and taken to where they were needed, manned by volunteers, usually drawn from the engineer's department.

A new staff grade introduced in 1903 was motor driver, made necessary when the North Eastern started its first motor bus service from Beverley to Brandesburton, North Frodingham and Beeford in the East Riding of Yorkshire.

The North Eastern and the Hull & Barnsley companies amalgamated in 1922 in readiness for the impending grouping at the end of the year. The Hull & Barnsley was more a South Yorkshire railway than a North East railway, although in LNER days many of its engines were at work in the North East, displaced from their native heath by ex-ROD 2-8-0 locomotives of Great Central design. A number of these Hull & Barnsley 0-6-0s were employed between Whitby and Malton and this view shows a typical train on that line in the 1930s, with the engine blasting away on a horsebox and four North Eastern bogie coaches. This section of line between Grosmont and Pickering is now operated by a preservation trust as a tourist line using steam and diesel motive power. (Locomotive & General Railway Photographs.)

Later the company developed an extensive network of bus services around Durham, and for years operated day and half-day tours based on Bridlington, Scarborough, Whitby and Harrogate, using char-a-bancs, with the seats rising in tiers, so that passengers in the rear seats required a ladder to reach them! The North Eastern also used a small fleet of steam wagons for country goods delivery and collection services, but these steamers were not really successful on the poor roads of 75 years ago! Road passenger services were transferred to associated companies in the 1920s and early 1930s, but the country goods services were developed, especially as wayside stations began to be closed from 1930. Rail closures were not the sole prerogative of Dr. Beeching in the 1960s!

For many years it was the practice to photograph locomotives with the crew and such photographs usually had a limited circulation among the men concerned, but in this day and age it has become fashionable to photograph locomotives with no human being in sight, be it footplate staff, shed staff, or even fellow enthusiasts. I feel that because of this much human interest has been lost; engines needed crews so why not photograph them? Many a time I look at a photograph of a group on or around a locomotive, and wonder what happened to them. Were they married, had they a family, what did they think of their job, what was their pay, what did they think of the locomotives with which they were provided, what was their housing like? There were so many more things which are a part of their social history. Railways were not simply locomotives and trains!

To help remedy this scarcity I have tried to choose photographs which show the staff, the lifeblood of any railway, be they footplate crews, permanent way men, signalmen, works staff, motor drivers, or staff from the head office at York.

The effects of the Beeching Plan, modernisation, and rationalisation have played havoc with railways in the North East, not least in buildings. Many stations have been demolished, or are now used for other purposes; locomotive sheds have almost disappeared, goods sheds are vanishing as traffic is concentrated at fewer depots, signalboxes have been decimated, and coal cells have been slaughtered. Items peculiar to railway operation — turntables, water cranes, coaling plants and the like are almost non-existent, while many bridges have gone where a line closure made it worthwhile to demolish bridges to recover scrap metal. Docks have been closed and are derelict, following the canals into obscurity.

What about the other side of the coin? Less than a handful of new stations have appeared, usually small structures to serve housing development in particular areas; better facilities have appeared at some of the larger stations, and much improved rolling stock has been produced to woo travellers from private cars and buses. Signalling and track improvements have been carried out to obtain higher speeds and shorter journey times, in some cases to compete with air travel. But does everyone want higher speeds, and increased fares to pay for them? Certainly there are operating benefits with better use of stock in the working day.

Railways in the North East have certainly seen change; after the graceful designs of NER locomotives, taking a hand in the East Coast partnership, came the glorious speed exploits of the LNER Pacifics, then the purely functional 'Deltic' diesels which brought everyday 100mph running, and now the High Speed Trains streaking along the beautifully aligned NER main line north of York at 125 mph. The NER was among the electrification pioneers with its Tyneside suburban lines, de-electrified by BR in the 1960s, only to be re-electrified in the late 1970s as a pioneer British rapid transit railway running underground below Newcastle. The NER would have been proud of it!

York, Newcastle & Berwick Railway.
York & North Midland Railway,
and Leeds Northern Railway.

General Order
Nº 19.

Traffic Manager's Office.

York November 15th 1853.

EAGLESCLIFFE JUNCTION STATION.

Notice is hereby given that the Station on the Leeds Northern extension, hitherto designated Eaglescliffe Junction Station, will hereafter be designated Preston Junction "for Middlesbro' and Redcar", and will be so named in the time tables of next month. (Yarm is the proper place to which Eaglescliffe passengers should be booked, the small village of Eaglescliffe being close to the Town of Yarm.

A Sherriff

General Manager of Traffic.

The three major companies which combined to form the North Eastern Railway in 1854 worked closely together before the formal amalgamation, as shown in this 1853 notice.

Eaglescliffe station had been opened in the previous year by the Leeds Northern Railway where its Northallerton — Stockton line crossed the Stockton & Darlington Railway on the level. The station name reverted to Eaglescliffe in 1878.

A.C. Sherriff became passenger manager of the North Eastern on its formation in 1854 but he resigned from the company's service in 1856. He was later elected Member of Parliament for Worcester and he became a director of several railway companies, including the Metropolitan and the Metropolitan District. He is commemorated by the derelict shaft of Sherriff's Pit, a once thriving ironstone mine on the Rosedale mineral branch in North Yorkshire, in an area which he helped to develop in the 1850s.

The date and location of this group photograph is unknown but it was probably taken in the Newcastle area in the early 1890s. The engine, No 164, is a Fletcher BTP 0-4-4T of 1878, which was rebuilt as an 0-6-0T in 1921 and continued to run until 1933. The group appears to consist of drivers, firemen and shed staff. Note the apparent youth of the figure third from the left standing on the running plate. (J.W. Armstrong collection)

Below: As there were so many men away in the armed forces in World War I women were employed in increasing numbers by the railway companies, not only in the usual clerical jobs, but on cleaning engines and other dirty tasks. This is a group of female cleaners at Neville Hill shed, Leeds, photographed on R1 4-4-0 1242 in 1916. Their working dress of trousers and long jacket was considered very attractive and elicited appreciative comments from the men!

This view was probably taken about the same time as that of 164, with the driver and fireman of class E 0-6-0T 1144 posing with a pretty visitor, probably dressed in her Sunday best. If she is still alive she must now be about 90 years of age! The engine is in the T.W. Worsdell livery which was discarded by his brother, Wilson, in 1894.

1 ENGINES AND MEN-AND WOMEN

This class Q 4-4-0 standing near the coal stage at West Hartlepool shed is also posed with a group of female cleaners. Note the cleanliness of the engine, and in particular the wheels and smokebox.

To use a modern term the railways were 'labour intensive'. North Road works opened in 1863 with a staff of about 150 men, but by the time these two views were taken in 1911 it had increased to 2,250. Additions to the buildings had been made over the years and the large erecting shop was opened in 1903 but only a corner of the shop appears in this view. The output target at that time was 580 engines repaired and overhauled each year, together with 40 new engines. The works commenced building diesel-electric locomotives in 1952 and in its 103 years' existence built 2,269 steam and 506 diesel locomotives, before closure in April 1966.

Wanted to purchase several new, or very good second hand locomotive engines of strong build and suitable for heavy mineral traffic. Replies to Samuel Chester, General Manager's Office, West Hartlepool Harbour & Railway, West Hartlepool).
(Railway Times 18 February 1854)

For sale at Durham on behalf of Richard Cail, who is retiring from the contract business, on Monday 11 April 1859. At the Passenger Railway Station, Durham, earth wagons etc. and at Dearness Railway Junction, rails, 290 earth wagons etc, and six-wheel locomotive and tender.
(Railway Times 2 April 1859)

Power for machines at North Road was provided by a stationary steam engine, driving shafts, from which individual machines were driven by leather belts. This is a view of the small machine shop, with all the work at a standstill while the photograph was taken. These are two of a series of views taken throughout the works.

South Durham & Lancashire Union Railway. An engine owned by Boulton & Co (contractors for the Stainmore section) conveyed a party from Barras, over Mousegill viaduct, to Bowesgate, where an incomplete bridge necessitated a change of engines. A fresh engine with a carriage to Lartington, joining a Stockton & Darlington engine and carriage conveying the directors etc. Both trains stopped on Tees viaduct and three cheers were given, then continuing to Barnard Castle where the monthly meeting was held, followed by a dinner at the Kings Head Inn.
(Railway Times 6 October 1860)

The last steam locomotive to be built at North Road was this BR Class 3 2-6-2T, No 84029, turned out in June 1957. The group in front of the engine includes the works manager, the assistant works manager, the chief boiler shop foreman, the chief erecting shop foreman, various foremen, assistant foremen, and three chargehands from the new engine pits. (British Railways)

Report on a claim for compensation from the NER by a 26 year old tea and coffee merchant. He was advised to go to Scarborough to recuperate after an accident on the North Eastern. It was alleged that he spent a lot of time at the George Hotel night after night getting drunk on whisky and being taken home by the hotel boots and carried upstairs to bed! A young women called by the defendants said the plaintiff had visited her constantly during his stay at Scarborough! He was awarded £25 to cover the expenses of his Scarborough visit. (Railway Times 4 April 1868)

The first 319 diesel locomotives built at Darlington were shunters but the first main line diesel appeared as D5094 in January 1960, a BR Type 2, again photographed with a group of staff responsible for its construction. (British Railways)

Funeral of Queen Victoria 2 February 1901: all railway business suspended. Goods and mineral service entirely discontinued. Passenger service as on a Sunday. At the hour of the funeral (2-3pm) all movement must cease for 10 minutes. Trains to be brought to a stand and remain motionless, and every servant on duty to stand quietly and reverently in his place for the period named. (NER Notice issued 31 January 1901).

Top right: Welded rails have been laid in increasing numbers over the last 25 years and here are two 600ft lengths of rail being unloaded and dropped into pre-stressed concrete sleepers. The far ends of the rails are securely anchored and as the train slowly moves forward the rails are guided into the baseplates as they slide off the end of the wagon. (British Railways)

Bottom right: On country branches the permanent way staff were issued with three-wheeled velocipedes and this one was used on the Malton-Driffield line in the 1930s. Note the tablet in its pouch hanging on the front of the machine, as the authority for it to occupy the single line.

Permanent way staff

Below: In May 1936 the position of the third rail on the Tyneside electrified system was changed from 19¼in from the nearest rail to a new British standard of 16in. The work was carefully planned so that it could be carried out over a single week-end, and all 72 miles of third rail were moved, using eight gangs with 30 men in each. Work commenced on Friday 22 May and was completed 45 minutes ahead of schedule on Monday 25 May; electrical and running tests followed and at 9.0pm the same evening the lines were ready for traffic. The more important lines were closed to electric trains on the Sunday and Monday, when the service was provided by steam hauled trains. The electric service on the north bank of the Tyne commenced on 29 March 1904 and the last electric trains ran on 17 June 1967 with a diesel multiple-unit service in replacement. Now some of the Tyneside lines are being re-electrified on 1,500V dc overhead system as part of the Tyne & Wear Metro.

A task which devolved upon the permanent way staff was the clearance of snow off the track, using only shovels and muscles, although where possible large snowploughs propelled by up to three locomotives were used. Stainmore Summit, 1,370ft above sea level, was always one of the first places on the old NER system to be blocked if there was a heavy snowfall; this 1952 view shows a gang at work clearing the way for a stranded train. Five years earlier, in the severe winter of 1947, this line was blocked for seven weeks as snowploughs could not force their way through the deep drifts. Jet engines were used in an experiment to see if they could blow the snow off the track, but they blew away the ballast as well! Unless securely anchored, the wagons on which the engine and fuel supplies were carried were pushed along the track by the power of the jet and the experiment was not a success. These troubles ceased when the Stainmore line closed in January 1962.

In January 1910 the 6.20pm Blackhill to Darlington train was held up at Rowley (near Consett) from 6.53pm on Friday, 28 January, to 4.30pm on the following Sunday, 30 January, because the line ahead was blocked by snow. Two engines were at the head of the train, with the leading engine, a class 398 0-6-0, running tender first assisting the train engine, a 2-4-0.

Another line which soon became blocked by snow, because of its high and exposed position, was the Rosedale mineral branch in North Yorkshire. Here again the permanent way staff have been called upon to clear the line. The engine is a former Stockton & Darlington 0-6-0, a type used on the Rosedale branch for many years.

WEAR VALLEY

2 SIGNALBOXES AND SIGNALMEN

The art, if that is the correct word, of signals and signalling has changed almost out of recognition over the last 50 years, with colour-light signals and power signalboxes taking over the work of semaphore signals and manual lever frames. The North Eastern was early in the field with electro-pneumatic installations, especially in the first decade of the century, while the North Eastern Area of the LNER kept the territory in the forefront by the introduction not only of a number of colour-light installations in the 1930s but such developments as thumbswitch or push button control panels. You could leave semaphores behind at York and not see another over the 44 miles to Darlington, with new boxes at Poppleton Junction (later Skelton Junction), Alne, Sessay Wood (later Pilmoor), Thirsk, North-

allerton, Eryholme and Darlington South, replacing numerous manual boxes. There were also electric installations at Hull and Leeds before 1939, and although a start was made on converting York the task was not completed until after World War II.

Each of the three divisions into which the North Eastern was at one time divided, Northern, Central, and Southern, had its own design of signalbox, but today there are still a few non-standard boxes in use, some dating from the introduction of the block system in the 1870s. Even finials on the top of signal posts differed, but the Central Division did not favour finials and the post top was pyramidal.

It is only in the last 20 years or so that great inroads have been made into the long familiar North Eastern slotted post signal, at one time

so common throughout North East England. Lamps fixed on top of short posts, with red discs bearing a white cross on the face, can still be seen outside some signalboxes. These were 'fogging objects' and their disappearance from the signalmen's sight in a fog meant that the time was ripe for the permanent way men to be called out to 'fog' specified signals. Revolving disc signals at minor level crossings can still be found at a few locations in the North East, and, according to a BR drawing, renewals of this old type of signal were still taking place in the 1960s.

The large electro-pneumatic systems at Newcastle Central, disappeared in 1959 when a new all-electric box was opened. At York and Newcastle it is now difficult to locate the signalbox, where the staff never see the trains they are handling. There is none of the looking out for the tail lamp as in mechanical boxes, for the illuminated diagram shows the occupation of all track circuits and has eliminated that time-honoured important function of the signalman.

Signalboxes came in all shapes and sizes, from the small box with only four levers, used as an inter-mediate block post to break up a long section of line, and thus increase the capacity, to the 295 manual lever frame at York (Locomotive Yard), and the large electro-pneumatic installations at Newcastle and Hull. This view, taken in January 1950, shows signalmen J.R. Dixon and E. Mothersdale at work at Leeman Road box, York. This box, at the north end of the station, was opened in 1900 in connection with the provision of a new platform, No 14. The box was abolished in 1951, together with all the other boxes serving York station, when a new all-electric signalbox was opened, work on which had been delayed by World War II.
(British Railways)

Above left: What can happen to a box in ten days! This box at Wear Valley Junction, between Bishop Auckland and Crook, was closed on 18 June 1969 and this is how it appeared ten days later, after vandals had broken almost every pane of glass!
(G. R. Foster)

The boxes controlling the traffic at Newcastle Central station were converted to electro-pneumatic operation in 1906 to 1910, the largest being Newcastle No 1 at the east end of the station. This box controlled the entrance to ten platforms off the four lines from the north, and from the three over the High Level Bridge, which converge at the famous crossing, often quoted as 'the largest crossing in the world'.
(C. Myton)

Lingdale box had a life of less than ten years, from 1912 to 1921! It was situated on the Kilton Mines branch and controlled the junction to Lingdale Mines, two of the Cleveland ironstone mines supplying the raw material required for the blast furnaces at nearby Middlesbrough.

With the opening of the new main line southwards from York, through Selby, in 1871 the North Eastern made a connection with the Great Northern at Shaftholme Junction, four miles north of Doncaster. Here there was for many years a small wooden signalbox owned by the Great Northern, although all the running expenses were paid by the North Eastern, the box having been erected for the latter's convenience. The photograph shows the new steel framed box built in 1958.

At the opposite end of the North Eastern, 175 miles to the north, was this box at Berwick, situated at the north end of the Royal Border Bridge and controlling the entry to Berwick station, which was North British property. Under LNER ownership Berwick was included in the North Eastern Area and the boundary with the Scottish Area was at Marshall Meadows, almost a mile to the north of the station. The complete rebuilding of the station was authorised in 1924 and included in the scheme was a new signalbox, making the old NER box redundant when the new station was opened in 1927.

(Locomotive & General Railway Photographs)

Miscellaneous services

Left: In 1957 the North Eastern Region of British Railways brought into use a rail mounted bridge inspection unit and this proved extremely useful for difficult locations such as the underside of arches. The unit was demonstrated to the press and television at Knaresborough, on the viaduct across the River Nidd. (British Railways)

Right: This Merryweather horse-drawn steam fire engine was NER No 1 and it carried the company's coat-of-arms on the side panels below the seats for the crew.

Below: A similar engine was based at Darlington North Road station, part of which can be seen in the background. The crew were volunteers from the staff, and although formed to fight fires on the company's property, and on adjoining property where the fire threatened NER buildings, they were allowed to help town brigades, provided a request for assistance was submitted in writing!

3 ROAD TRANSPORT

The tiered seats on the early char-a-bancs were inconvenient, especially for ladies wearing the long and voluminous skirts of the period, and there was no protection from the weather. However, competition from other operators with newer vehicles resulted in the NER modernising its fleet with 'torpedo' bodies, having all the seats on the same level, with side doors, and a hood which could be raised to cover all the passengers if and when it rained. This is a rebodied Fiat at Scarborough station forecourt in 1913. Similar tours are still run from this very spot but now operated by United Automobile Services.

For its char-a-banc services the North Eastern built up a fleet of Durkopp, Fiat, Hallford and Saurer vehicles, purchasing the chassis and building the bodies at York carriage works. This Hallford chara was photographed at Kirby Moorside about 1910. The bodies were interchangeable and in the winter months a van or lorry body was fitted and the vehicle used on goods delivery work.

This Leyland vehicle was introduced in September 1912; the chassis cost £662 complete with lamps and tyres. This was one of the vehicles requisitioned by the government in World War I, when it was fitted with a lorry body for military service. It is seen here on a staff outing from the North Eastern's headquarters at York.

Steam road wagons were introduced in 1904 and vehicles from different makers were purchased to find which was the most suitable. Most popular were the Straker and Londonderry wagons and seven of each were purchased. This is the initial Londonderry wagon, registration number BT 204 and NER No 6; subsequent lorries were fitted with a canopy over the driver and mate. However, the NER eventually pinned its faith on petrol driven vehicles. (British Railways)

The North Eastern developed a very extensive bus service around Durham City but this network was taken over by United in 1930. This Leyland bus (DN 6058 and NER 109) ended its days at Hull in 1933, in use as an engineer's department service vehicle; here it is in pristine condition on a trial run from the road motor engineer's workshops at York. Although authorised in 1921 the bus was not registered until October 1923 and, apparently, was turned out carrying NER livery. (British Railways)

Three Garrett steam tractors were obtained by the North Eastern, BT 210 in 1906, BT 364 in 1907, and DN 4581 in 1921. They were used for hauling heavy loads. Inflation was rife in those days and although BT 364 cost £528 in 1907, DN 4581 cost £1,128 14 years later. According to NER records Garrett engines were preferred because Sir George Gibb, general manager of the North Eastern, was related by marriage to the Garrett family! Wheels within wheels! (British Railways)

In 1922 NER 110 (for which no registration number has been traced) was fitted with rail wheels and used on local services in the York area. In 1923 it was replaced by a larger railcar and transferred to Selby, where it ran until destroyed by fire in November 1926.

4 STOCKTON & DARLINGTON RAILWAY

Ask any non-railway enthusiast, who invented the steam locomotive, and the answer will almost certainly be George Stephenson; the name of his first engine, the Rocket, and the name of the railway, the Stockton & Darlington!

Certainly George Stephenson engineered the Stockton & Darlington, but there were many other railways in use before the Quaker line came into being; certainly Stephenson produced the Rocket, but for the Liverpool & Manchester Railway and not the Stockton & Darlington. It was his Locomotion that worked the inaugural train on the Stockton & Darlington in 1825!

The Stockton & Darlington's claim to fame rests on the fact that it was the first steam worked railway to provide public transport, although it must be admitted that for the first few years the passengers were carried in horse drawn coaches, and only the more important coal traffic was conveyed in chaldron wagons hauled by steam locomotives, if and when the steam locomotives were working satisfactorily. Like many other new inventions there were teething troubles with the engines and they posed a lot of problems, especially to Timothy Hackworth, who was entrusted with the herculean task of keeping them in working order.

The eventual success of the Stockton & Darlington lay mainly in the fact that it was controlled to a large extent by members of the Pease family, which had the welfare of the line at heart, backed up by other Quaker families in the Darlington and Yarm areas.

Running east and west the Stockton & Darlington was crossed by the North Eastern's main line at Darlington, where there were two stations, North Road on the Stockton & Darlington, and Bank Top on the North Eastern. Although there was a connecting service between the two it was not until 1887 that trains from the former Stockton & Darlington line could use the North Eastern station. I say 'former Stockton & Darlington' because the NER absorbed the pioneer company in 1863, although for more than ten years the Stockton & Darlington Committee had almost complete autonomy over its line, subject only to NER control where large expenditure was involved.

The first accommodation provided by the S&DR for its passengers was in the goods warehouse adjoining the turnpike road to Durham where it passed over the railway on the northern outskirts of Darlington, but in 1842 this building was replaced by a custom built station a short distance to the west. The building was extended at various times to

The exterior of North Road station, built in 1842 and renovated in 1975 in connection with the 150th anniversary of the opening of the Stockton & Darlington Railway. The rooms on the ground floor now have displays of small railway items, photographs etc, with the former train shed accommodating locomotives and rolling stock.

The upper floor is a later addition and the portico originally had six columns and five bays; the left-hand bay and the end column were added at an unknown date, presumably to provide covered access to the double doors on the left.

provide additional office accommodation but neglect by British Railways, and its demotion to an unstaffed station, left it open to vandalism and it became little more than a ruin.

However, in the 1970s, with the impending celebrations to mark the 150th anniversary of the opening of the Stockton & Darlington, a determined effort was made to save this historic building and to use it as a museum. Co-operation between volunteers led to the formation of a trust, and with the backing of Darlington Borough Council the station was restored and renovated in time for its formal opening by the Duke of Edinburgh on 27 September 1975, 150 years to the day since George Stephenson had stood on the swaying footplate of Locomotion as it trundled slowly from Shildon to Stockton, hauling wagons of coal and a primitive coach carrying the directors of the railway company, not to mention the many members of the public obtaining a free ride on top of the coal.

Over the years people with foresight have preserved items of interest connected with the Stockton & Darlington Railway, over which Locomotion worked the first train on 27 September 1825. The Stockton & Darlington itself decided to preserve Locomotion and from 1857 it was placed on a stone plinth outside North Road station in Darlington. In 1892 it was moved to Bank Top station in the same town, where it could be under cover, and six years later it was joined by another old engine, Derwent.

In 1975 both engines were moved to the new museum at North Road station, which utilises the train shed of the 1842 building. Trains on the Darlington-Bishop Auckland service actually stop at a platform adjoining the Museum, in what was originally the carriage shed. (N.E. Stead)

COPY

Stockton and Darlington Railway,
Secretary's Office.

Darlington, May 20, 1857

Dear Sir,

The Directors have it in contemplation to erect a suitable Pedestal, &c at Darlington upon which to place the Old Locomotive Engine No 1, as a memento of the past, and they think the laying of the Foundation Stone a fitting time to give an Entertainment to the Company's Agents in the several departments, as far as they can be dispensed with from their duties. On the list furnished of those likely to be able to attend, is your name; and this is to inform you that the day fixed for the occasion is Saturday the 6th of June. The following will be the order of proceeding, at which it is hoped you will be present

At one o'clock the foundation Stone will be laid by Edward Pease Esq

At two o'clock the Agents Dinner will be ready at the Sun Inn Darlington

After which the Agents will (through the kindness of J Pease Esq M.P) have the liberty to visit the Grounds &c at Pierremont

Trains for East and West will leave the Darlington Station in the Evening

I remain,

Yours very truly,

Tho' Mac Nay

To Mr.

N.B. A Ticket will be forwarded to you on application to this office, which will admit to the grounds and to the dinner

Locomotion plinth invitation.

Below: Photographs of Hackworth type locomotives at work are very scarce for they went to the scrap-heap in the 1860s at a period when railway photography was in its infancy. In any case these engines ended their days in the remote moorland district around Waskerley in North-west Durham. This view of Stanhope was probably taken in that area. The engine was a sister engine to Derwent, both built by W & A Kitching in 1845.

The drivers on this class of engine were the lowest paid, receiving only 5d (2½p) compared with the top rate of 7½d (3½p) per hour paid to drivers working goods trains between Barnard Castle and Penrith with modern engines.

Right upper: Derwent also stands on the platform at North Road station. It was built in 1845 at the nearby workshops of William and Alfred Kitching, who were closely connected with the Stockton & Darlington Railway. Their father had an ironmonger's shop in Darlington and after supplying the new company with nails and other small items they decided to build a foundry with the object of making and supplying equipment for the new form of transport. Derwent was of a type favoured by Timothy Hackworth, the locomotive chief of the Stockton & Darlington, having two tenders, that at the back carrying the water, and that at the chimney end carrying the coal, for these engines were fired at the front end. (N E Stead)

Right lower: Hackworth's successor, William Bouch, built a more conventional type of 0-6-0, although he did favour the 'long boiler' design with a deep firebox behind the rear axle. He also had a preference for the dome being placed just behind the chimney, on the front ring of the boiler barrel.

This engine, built by R & W Hawthorn in 1868, had Bouch's system of feed water heating, with a water jacket surrounding the chimney; note the gauge glass on the side of the chimney, with a protecting sight screen ahead of it. Another Bouch fitting was the steam brake acting on the intermediate and rear coupled wheels.

Note also the two sets of buffers, the lower set for use with chaldron wagons, where the long wooden frame members were extended at each end to form buffers. This engine was not withdrawn until 1908, by which time it had received a Worsdell pattern boiler.

Over the years the North Eastern absorbed its competitors in the North East. Of these the West Hartlepool Harbour & Railway (taken over in 1865) had been formed by various earlier amalgamations and included the Clarence Railway and the Stockton & Hartlepool Railway. The WHHR was a mainly coal carrying line, shipping the coal at staiths at West Hartlepool. This view shows 0-4-0T Alexandra renumbered into NER stock, with the raised approach track to one of the staiths in the background.

5 OTHER INDEPENDENTS

The Blyth & Tyne was another line whose staple traffic was coal. Set in South-east Northumberland the line's chief object in life was to carry coal down to the Tyne for shipment, although in 1864 the company built a line westwards to reach Newcastle.

As might be expected the company had a fleet of 0-6-0 tender engines for mineral traffic and this one, originally B&T No 35, was built at its Percy Main shops in 1868. The Blyth & Tyne was taken over by the North Eastern in 1874.

Back in County Durham, the Earl of Londonderry built a harbour at Seaham, south of Sunderland, in 1831 and this handled shipment of coal from his Lordship's pits. In fact coal production was so high that it could not all be handled at Seaham Harbour and consequently in 1854 a line was opened northwards to Sunderland to utilise the docks there.

Again, although primarily a coal carrying line, the railway carried passengers in trains usually worked by 2-4-0T engines.
(J.W. Armstrong collection)

Below: The sister engine built in 1856 became NER 2269, and it was photographed carrying that number while shunting at Scarborough in the early years of this century. The Londonderry Railway was taken over by the North Eastern in 1900 and subsequently incorporated into the West Hartlepool-Sunderland coast line.

Below: William Barningham of Albert Hill Ironworks, Darlington, built locomotives for his own use
and this is an 0-6-0T of uncertain date but probably
built around 1870. Its similarity to the John Harris
engine suggests there may have been some connection between the two concerns, and it also
appears possible that this engine started life as a
0-4-0T.

Top left: A John Harris locomotive of about 1863.

On account of the heavy cost of conveying coal
to Pateley Bridge the old town has not yet been
lighted with gas and candles are still burnt in
the lamps in the town streets.
(Railway Times 7 September 1861)

Bottom left: An I'Anson 0-4-0T built in 1875 for a
Darlington ironworks. It ended its days in a Wear
shipyard, having survived two world wars!

In 1935 Robert Stephenson & Co built this large Kitson-Meyer 2-8-8-2T for the Colombian National Railways.

Because of lack of space for expansion at Newcastle Robert Stephenson & Co moved to new works at Darlington in 1900 and the first engine was produced in 1902. Much of the work was on engines for overseas, but some B17 4-6-0 engines were built for the LNER in 1936/7. No 2870 was named after the football team Tottenham Hotspur, but in September 1937 it was fitted with a streamlined covering and renamed City of London for working the 'East Anglian' express between Norwich and London (Liverpool Street).

Stephenson & Co also built numerous diesel-electric locomotives for British Railways, the last being D6898 in 1963. Unfortunately the works closed in the following year.

Another firm closely connected with the Stockton & Darlington Railway was Gilkes, Wilson of Middlesbrough which became (through amalgamation) Hopkins, Gilkes in 1865, and lasted in that form until 1880. Between 1865 and 1875 the company turned out a number of 0-6-0 engines for the Darlington Section of the NER, but it also constructed a number of 0-4-0PTs for industrial use. These had a pair of vertical cylinders reminiscent of some of Hackworth's early engines for the Stockton & Darlington.

Locomotive repairers also established themselves in the North east, a Darlington concern being John F. Wake, whose premises were adjacent to the East Coast main line south of Darlington. He was particularly active prior to World War I and he supplied to the War Department (for use at Catterick Camp) a couple of engines he had purchased from the NER and renovated. One was a class 964A 0-6-0T, which had started life in 1875 as a saddle-tank.

Black, Hawthorn & Co commenced trading in Gateshead in 1865 and they supplied numerous locomotives to railways in this country and overseas. Their British customers were usually industrial concerns purchasing 0-4-0Ts, and 0-6-0Ts, but the North Eastern, probably supporting local industry, ordered five class 964 0-6-0STs in 1872 and a further five in 1873. No 780 was the last of the 1872 batch. Incidentally, a further 40 of this class were built by Robert Stephenson & Co in 1873-5. Many of the class were sold to colliery and dock companies in the North east and one continued to run at Seaham Harbour until 1963.

Robert Stephenson & Co amalgamated with R & W Hawthorn, Leslie & Co Ltd in 1937, the new company being known as Robert Stephenson & Hawthorn Ltd. Hawthorn, Leslie's works were at Forth Banks in Newcastle, where George Stephenson had set up the locomotive building works for his son Robert in 1823. Under the new arrangement both the Darlington and the Forth Banks works continued to build locomotives, the smaller engines usually being built at Newcastle, including this 0-6-0PT built for the Western Region of BR in 1950.

Above: In 1919 Sir W G Armstrong Whitworth & Co Ltd of Scotswood obtained an order from the North Eastern for 50 class T2 0-8-0 engines at £8,000 each, and later an order for 25 class E1 0-6-0T engines at £6,950 each. The firm continued to build steam locomotives but in the early 1930s began to concentrate more on diesel locomotives and railcars. This view shows one of the E1 engines for the NER, which became class J72 on the LNER.

Below: A stranger on the North Eastern in 1860 was this Kitson built 4-4-0 for Chile, which was given a trial run between Leeds and Harrogate.

Top right: The Earl of Durham's Railway developed from the wagonways built in the late 18th and early 19th centuries to obtain economical transport of coal from the pits to the River Wear in the Fatfield area. As traffic increased and ships grew larger it was necessary to obtain loading facilities nearer the sea and the coal was worked to Sunderland, at first almost wholly over rope-worked inclines. In the 1860s it became possible to work to Sunderland with locomotives, using the NER line from Penshaw to Pallion, and then the branch down to Lambton staiths. For this comparatively long run six-coupled tender engines were necessary, some of which were built in the railways' own workshops at Philadelphia. This is one of the local products, No 9 built in 1877, which survived to become National Coal Board property in 1947.

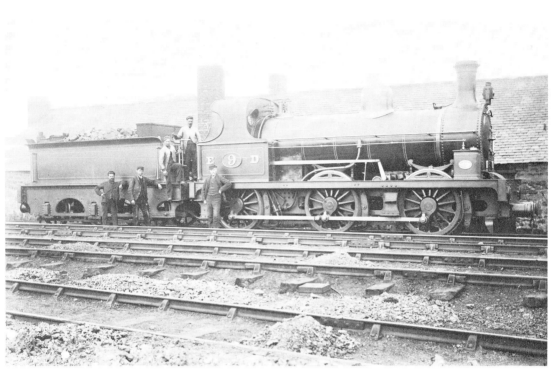

Below: From Penshaw to Cox Green Junction there were four tracks, with the coal trains using the southern pair. Large 0-6-2T engines replaced the 0-6-0s and here is No 5 (now preserved) waiting to pass on to the double track section after a BR Sunderland-Durham train has cleared the junction. (Ian S Carr)

7 ROLLING STOCK AND BRIDGES

The North Eastern was famous for its Bain clerestory roofed coaches, which replaced the large fleet of four- and six-wheel coaches from 1895, until eventually there were clerestory coaches with many different combinations of compartments and toilets. From 1905, when the NER introduced autocars, 36 clerestory coaches were fitted with driving controls so that they could operate push-and-pull services with Fletcher BTP 0-4-4T engines.

One of these autocar coaches, which could easily be distinguished by their two 'portholes' at the driving end, has survived and it is currently being restored by the North Eastern Railway Coach Group. This is the vehicle concerned, here as E23453, in use as an ordinary brake composite, photographed at Scarborough. (W A Camwell)

Some of the redundant four-wheel vehicles were used in collision and telescoping tests at York carriage works in April 1911 and one of these tests ended with a luggage van mounting a couple of wagons! (British Railways)

In 1906 a change was made to an elliptical roof, often with a body identical to the clerestory roof version. Lavatory composite 2009 (to Diagram 122 introduced in 1906) had a layout exactly the same as the clerestory lavatory composite to Diagram 5, of which 138 were built between 1896 and 1905. (British Railways)

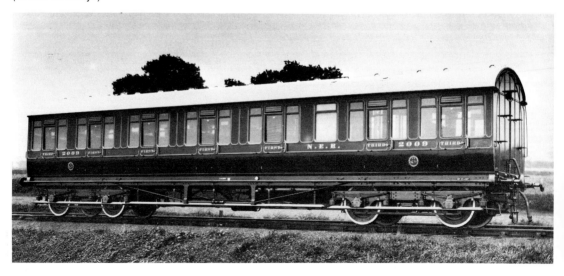

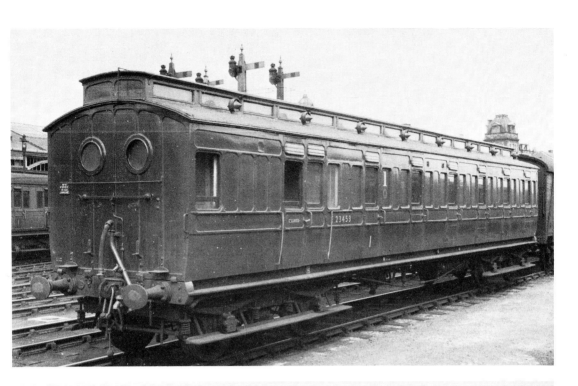

Below: The first corridor stock was introduced in 1908 for use on Newcastle-Liverpool trains, although similar stock had been in use on East Coast Joint Stock workings for some years. This open first No 1855 was built in 1914, taking the number of a clerestory roofed dining car sold to the North British Railway in 1913. (British Railways)

Right: Interior of NER open first No 1855. (British Railways)

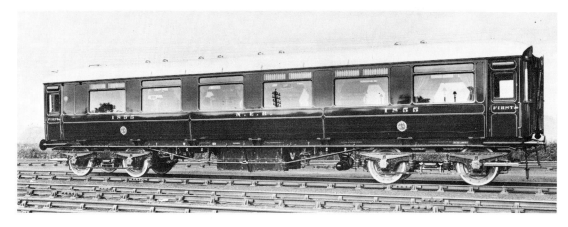

Right: Three Pullman sleeping cars were used on the East Coast services, Columba, India and Iona; India was destroyed in the Manor House collision in 1892, but the other two were incorporated into the ECJS fleet in 1895, Iona eventually passing into Great Northern ownership, and Columba into North Eastern ownership. This unique interior view was found with some photographs of a snowbound train at Acklington in March 1886 and probably shows passengers in the Pullman car on the stranded train, with the conductor about to serve a warming cup of tea or coffee! (C B Foster collection)

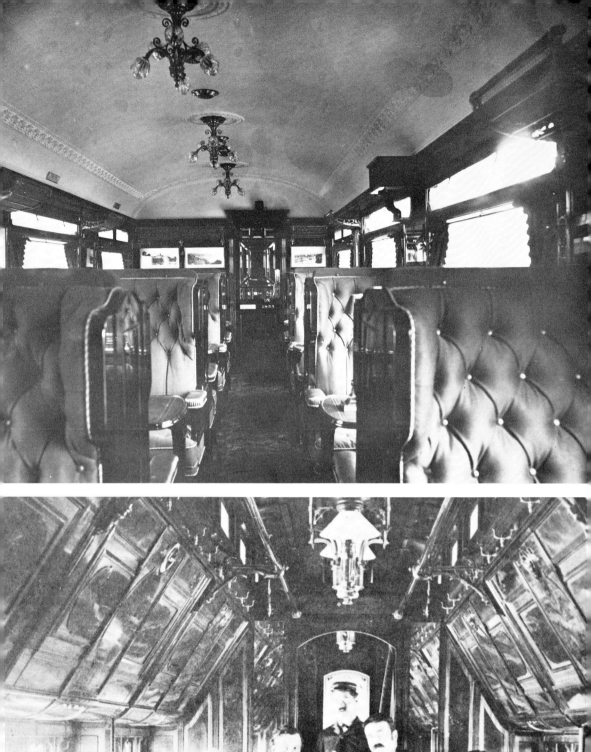

Railways across rivers and valleys require bridges and the early railway companies had to be prepared to build plenty of bridges to obtain a level and direct route. Stone was almost invariably used for construction in the early days, although George Stephenson designed the cast iron bridge across the River Gaunless at West Auckland for the opening of the Stockton & Darlington Railway in 1825.

One of the most notable stone viaducts in the north is the Royal Border Bridge at Berwick, opened by Queen Victoria on 29 August 1850. It took more than three years to build, and it still stands astride the Tweed valley between Tweedmouth and Berwick, carrying all East Coast traffic. The treble thickness pier on the Northumbrian side of the Tweed was built to act as a central abutment, so that the bridge could be erected on both sides of it simultaneously. (Locomotive & General Railway Photographs)

A contemporary stone viaduct to the Royal Border Bridge was that at Yarm carrying the Leeds Northern's extension from Northallerton to Stockton, opened in 1852. (British Railways)

Cast iron tubular viaducts were used at Upgang, Newholm Beck, East Row, Sandsend and Staithes on the Whitby, Redcar & Middlesbrough Union Railway between Whitby and Loftus.

The WRMU line was closed in 1958 and all five viaducts were subsequently demolished. This the largest of the five, at Staithes, in course of demolition, with one of the piers just falling. The columns were hollow and to provide extra strength they were filled with concrete.
(British Railways)

Because of the navigable rivers crossed by the North Eastern and its constituents, a number of swing bridges were provided, particularly across rivers flowing into the Humber. At Hull the York & North Midland Railway built a single line swing bridge across the River Hull to give access to Victoria Dock. In 1907 a new double track swing bridge was constructed alongside but trouble was experienced as it was being rolled into position when some of the wheels of the carrying bogies disintegrated under the weight. This view, taken during the rolling-in operation, shows a group surveying the damage!

The River Tyne has long been notable for its road and rail bridges joining Newcastle and Gateshead. From 1849 to 1906 there was only one rail bridge, namely Robert Stephenson's High Level, with three tracks to carry all the north-south traffic, not to mention the numerous light engines to and from Gateshead shed.

The High Level actually had two decks, the upper deck across the tops of the girders carrying the railway and the lower deck, suspended from the upper deck, carrying the roadway.

The low level swing bridge visible in the background replaced a stone arched road bridge in 1876. (British Railways)

In 1906, after four years work, a new bridge carrying four tracks was opened by King Edward VII and named after him. Not only did the bridge provide badly needed relief to the High Level but at last allowed East Coast trains to pass through Central station without reversing.

Although the King Edward bridge was formally opened on 10 July 1906 it was not until almost three months later that it was opened for regular traffic. This view shows the first train crossing the bridge on the misty morning of 1 October 1906; the train was the 9.30am from Newcastle to York and the Great Central line headed by Class Q 4-4-0 1930.

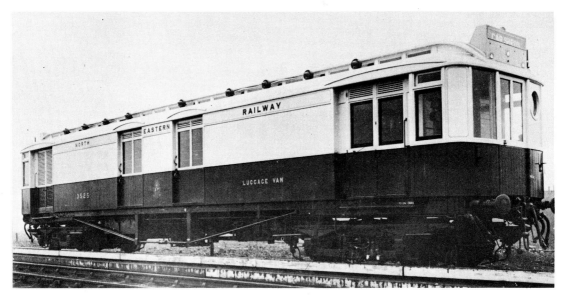

Above: For its Tyneside electric trains inaugurated in March 1904 the North Eastern adopted a distinctive red and cream livery. In addition to the normal passenger vehicles there were three motor parcels vans for serving the stations on the electrified system; two of these were also used at times of pressure to handle a train of ten six-wheel coaches, with a motor parcels van at each end. Jumper cables were fitted throughout the train so that the driver of the leading van had control of the van in the rear. The practice continued with the new stock built by the LNER in 1937, but by then the ten six-wheel coaches had been replaced by six bogie vehicles.

Top right: in conjunction with electrification of the passenger carrying lines the goods branch from Manors to Newcastle Quayside was also electrified and two locomotives were built to work this steeply graded line. No 26500, originally NER No1, is seen at Quayside Yard awaiting its load to take up to Manors when the author made some footplate journeys on the line in 1957.

Right: On the Quayside itself the shunting was carried out by J71 and J72 0-6-0T engines. The bridge in the background is the Tyne Bridge opened in 1928, with the High Level Bridge just visible behind the crane on the right.

Another freight and mineral line to be electrified was that between Shildon and Newport (Middlesbrough), on which overhead catenary current collection at 1,500V dc was used. Most of the system was brought into use in 1915, although the final stretch, from Erimus to Newport East, was not completed until 1916. For this service ten 74ton electric locomotives were built at Darlington Works, and they proved to be extremely successful, hauling 1,400ton trains with ease, although the drivers had to be particularly careful in keeping trains under control when descending from Shildon with fully loaded mineral wagons.

At first the overhead wires were energised only from Shildon to Bowesfield West, where this view was taken on the occasion of a trial run with the first locomotive, No 3. Standing in the cab doorway is R J Robson, who was entrusted by Vincent Raven with much of the design work on these locomotives; Robson eventually became the Chief Locomotive Draughtsman (in 1920) and retired in 1932.

For the envisaged main line electrification scheme at 1,500 volts dc, Raven produced the unlucky No 13, which in its 28 years existence was used only on trial trips and demonstrations. It spent most of its time in the paint shop at North Road Works in Darlington, although it ended its days in store at South Gosforth electric car sheds before being sold for scrap in 1950.

... ordered that the passenger trains upon the Thirsk Branch be worked by means of a small engine, which will also be sufficient to work the goods, and that the Aerolite be got back for this purpose. (Leeds Northern Railway Minute 17 June 1852)

Mr. Cudworth reported that the old timber viaduct on the Cleveland Railway across Admiral Chaloner's land at Guisborough fell down during a recent gale. It was decided that the old viaduct should be removed from Admiral Chaloner's land.

(NER Minutes 10 March 1881)

The Tyneside electrification was abandoned in 1967 and the last trains ran on Saturday 17 June. A distinctive feature of the system was the small wooden platform and ramp placed at each signal where the drivers were required to use the signal-post telephone. These platforms were provided so that the driver could step out of his cab without the need to climb down to the ballast, where he might have stepped on to a live rail. This 8-car set forming the 16.57 Newcastle to Newcastle via Wallsend later formed the 18.15 from Newcastle, the last passenger carrying train over the system. (Ian S Carr)

On the evening of 7 August 1926 a collision occurred at Manors between a freight train and a driverless electric train. It was later discovered that while attempting to watch a couple in the leading saloon, the driver had been leaning out of the door when he struck the abutment of an overbridge and his body fell from the train. To keep the train running under power he had tied down the dead-man's handle on the controller with two handkerchiefs, as this view shows.

Reported that all trains on the Richmond branch can be worked by tank engines and it was recommended that a new turntable be not put down.
(NER Minutes 24 May 1877)

Above: North Eastern locomotives sometimes got themselves into some most awkward situations, providing hard and tricky work for the crews of the crane and tool vans. This is an ex Stockton & Darlington 0-6-0, wheels uppermost, at Lingdale Junction in November 1900, giving an excellent view of the motion without the need for an inspection pit!

9 ACCIDENTS

Top right: The engine was pulled upright using two sets of block and tackle, with two engines hauling in opposite directions away from one another. The tank engine in the right foreground is merely providing a deadweight to hold the track in place where the blocks have been anchored. One of the hauling engines, P1 0-6-0 2058, can be seen in the background, and beyond it is class 38 4-4-0 158 on an officers' saloon.

Right: A double-headed freight train was unable to stop when platelayers had a rail out between Gainford and Winston on the Darlington to Barnard Castle line and this was the result! This occurred in October 1905.

This class E 0-6-0T came to grief on the old Red-heugh incline in 1890 but the cause is unknown. The bridge is the Redheugh road bridge, and through the large brick arch can be seen one of the buildings of Gateshead Locomotive Works.

A shunting mishap at Heck, between Selby and Doncaster, in 1923. The wheels of the inverted wagon appear to have provided the means for the van to aspire to greater heights! The mishap was due to a signalman's error.

Below: In May 1914 at Tees Bridge, Thornaby, P3 1067 was returning to Carlisle when it was derailed, ran down the river bank, and finished in the Tees. As appears to have been usual in those days there were plenty of people prepared to stand (and sit) and stare!

Right: Class R 4-4-0 725 was derailed at Felling in March 1907 when the rails were buckled by the heat of the sun. Again a large number of idle spectators watch the rerailing operations, which required the use of two steam cranes. The engine was only three months old and it was working a train of LNWR stock on the Liverpool-Newcastle service, via Leeds and Sunderland.

Above: When a Selby driver on T2 0-8-0 2219 allowed the left big-end to run hot this was the result, a severely distorted crank-pin and lost brasses. This occurred in January 1922 and the driver concerned was reduced to a shunting driver for a year!

Damaged LNWR coaches, with a group of NER officials in the foreground after the Felling derailment. Once again plenty of spectators!

In this 1950 accident the WD 2-8-0 ran away from Neville Hill shed yard with no-one aboard. It negotiated Marsh Lane cutting, travelling west on an eastbound track, ran through Marsh Lane goods yard, and finally crashed through the boundary wall into the street. It was suspected that the engine had been deliberately set in motion but this was never confirmed.

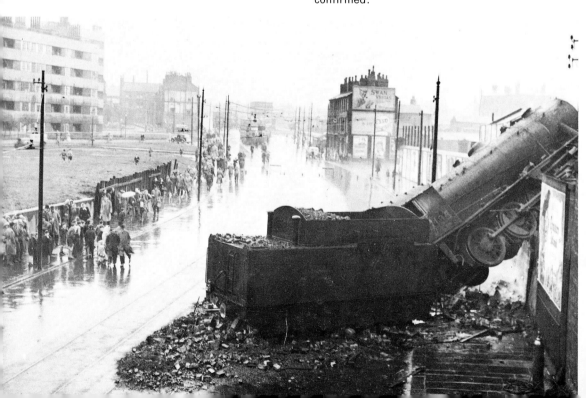

A familiar sight at wayside stations was the daily pick-up goods shunting the yard. This is at Hessle in the 1930s and the engine is J21 0-6-0 1590.

10 FREIGHT TRAFFIC

For its East Coast expresses the NER produced the first English 4-6-0 in 1899. However, these ten engines had only a short life on such trains as they were supplanted by a similar number of 4-4-2 engines in 1903/4 and henceforward used on express goods and excursion work. A further 30 Class S 4-6-0s were turned out from Gateshead in 1906-8, the last 20 to a modified design distinguishable by the narrow driving wheel splashers.

By 1938 there were only four still in service, all to the modified design and all stationed at Hull Dairycoates shed, Nos 738, 748, 753 and 759. This is 748 trundling through Selby and about to clatter over the swing bridge, on what looks like a load of empties from Gascoigne Wood to Hull. (E E Smith)

Left: By swallowing up the two companies which owned the docks at Hartlepool and West Hartlepool, now combined as Hartlepool, the North Eastern obtained a monopoly at the port, where the main traffics were the export of coal and the import of pit props for use in the extensive County Durham coalfield. (British Railways)

Bottom left: The North Eastern Railway owned the docks at the larger ports on the East Coast at Hull, Middlesbrough, the Hartlepools, and Tyne Dock, with the coal shipping staiths at Dunston and Blyth. The docks at Sunderland were owned by the River Wear Commissioners, while Tyne Dock passed into the hands of the Tyne Improvement Commission in May 1937. Tyne Dock was famous for the amount of coal it could handle but this view shows esparto grass, used in paper making, being unloaded. (British Railways)

Below: The first dock at Hull was opened in 1778; previously traffic had been handled on the banks of the River Hull. To form an arc of docks joining the River Hull and the River Humber, Humber Dock was opened in 1809 and Prince's Dock in 1829. Until 1893 these docks were owned by the Hull Dock Company. This is Prince's Dock, almost in the centre of the city, now redundant and derelict.

Out of gauge loads were common, such as this cast steel shaft bracket en route from Darlington Forge works to Stockton for shipment, in 1924. The extremities of the arms were 13ft from the centre of the wagon and a steam crane was in attendance to move the load when required to pass lineside structures. Such journeys were usually carried out on Sundays when traffic was light.

The NER owned a large fleet of small craft such as tugs, dredgers and lighters; this is the twin-screw tug William Gray at work in Union Dock at Hartlepool. The vessel was named after Sir William Gray, the founder of the Hartlepool shipbuilding firm of that name, who was a director of the North Eastern Railway from 1886 to 1898. (British Railways)

Locomotives from North Eastern builders were often shipped at Middlesbrough and on the Tyne, such as this Stephenson & Hawthorn product.

To get the coal to the port for shipment chaldron wagons were used, and although they went out of general use on the main-line railways towards the end of the nineteenth century they lingered on in collieries until the 1960s. This is a South Hetton Colliery wagon preserved by BR and photographed in 1953. (British Railways)

To carry coal economically and in the largest wagons generally acceptable in the North east the NER used a 20 ton hopper wagon, with bottom doors for unloading at coal staiths. This type proved so successful that many more were built in LNER days, such as 46254, constructed at Faverdale in 1925.

Having no side doors and no end doors these wagons were extremely strong, as proved by the condition of these 20-tonners after a shunting mishap.

The first Worsdell 4-4-0s for the North Eastern were the class F (compound) and F1 (simple) engines, which first appeared in 1887. No 1543 is standing in Platform 4 at Scarborough on a train of Great Northern stock, on what would most probably be a through train to Kings Cross — and the fore-runner of the 'Scarborough Flyer'. The engine is in its original (compound) state, in Wilson Worsdell livery, so it was probably taken about 1900; it was withdrawn from traffic in 1932.

11 LOCOMOTIVES IN THE NORTH EAST

The most successful class of North Eastern 4-4-0, class R, appeared from Gateshead Works in 1899 and a second batch of 30 was built in 1906/7. In the 1920s and 1930s, in the days of Atlantics and Pacifics on the expresses, the Class R engines worked the stopping trains on the main line and this is 1184 leaving Croft Spa on a Darlington-York slow. The photograph was taken in August 1924 and little has changed since NER days, the new 'L. & N.E.R.' livery of the engine and tender being the most noticeable feature. (W Rogerson)

The ultimate in 4-4-0s in the North Eastern Area was the D49 or 'Shire' class, which first appeared in 1927 to the designs of Gresley. No 320 Warwickshire is seen here entering West Hartlepool on a Liverpool-Newcastle train, with a North Eastern 12-wheel restaurant car as the leading vehicle, followed by two 8-wheel NE coaches. (W L Good)

The North Eastern Atlantics put up some good work on the LNER Pullman trains, for which they were well suited. One engine worked from Leeds to Newcastle and another north to Edinburgh. This is No 2211 passing Morpeth Level Crossing box on a down Pullman.

The Gresley Pacifics of Great Northern design eclipsed the Raven Pacifics of the North Eastern, and some of the Raven engines had a very short life, only 12 years in the case of this engine, 2402 City of York. The location is near Reston, north of Berwick, and the photographer C.J.L. Romanes, who lived at nearby Duns. (Locomotive & General Railway Photographs)

2-4-0 No 312 (later incorporated into class 25) is seen standing at the west end of Newcastle Central station about 1870. Part of the arched roof of the station can be seen on the left, while behind the engine is an engine shed which once existed at the west end of Central Station.

The Gresley Pacifics were impressive looking engines and first appeared at York working in from the Great Northern section. Later, of course, 15 of the class were allocated to Gateshead and Heaton sheds and became responsible for the heaviest main line workings performed by the two Tyneside sheds. Five of the class were allocated to the Scottish Area and they worked southwards to Newcastle, only rarely being seen south of the Tyne until 1928 when the non-stop 'Flying Scotsman' took Edinburgh engines through to London.

The ultimate in North Eastern Railway steam power. The pioneer Raven Pacific, 2400, photographed in the paint shop yard when new in December 1922. It was named City of Newcastle in 1924 but ran only until July 1936.

The ultimate in BR North Eastern Region steam power. The class A1 Pacifics were built at Doncaster and Darlington and this is the first of the Darlington series, 60130, later named Kestrel, built in September 1948. Because of dieselisation these fine engines had a life only a little longer than the Raven Pacifics and this particular engine was withdrawn in October 1965. (British Railways)

Of the 80 steam railcars purchased by the LNER from Sentinel Waggon Works Ltd between 1925 and 1932 58 worked in the North Eastern Area. The earliest cars had only two cylinders and were first turned out in brown livery and un-named. To gain publicity they were later named after stage coaches and to make them more noticeable they were painted red and cream, although this was later changed to green and cream. This view shows the second of the North Eastern Area cars, built in 1927 and put to work in the Newcastle area. It later received the name Brilliant and it ran until 1942. (British Railways)

The Sentinel cars were unusual for rail traction in having water tube boilers instead of the more common fire-tube type, but even more unusual was this 4-cylinder compound locomotive, designed by Gresley and built at Darlington works, although the water tube boiler itself was constructed by Yarrow & Co of Glasgow. The engine was built under conditions of secrecy and the nickname it received at the time, 'Hush-Hush', remained with it for many years. After 5½ years of tests, trials, and modifications it was stored out of use from mid-1935 until it was rebuilt with a normal locomotive type boiler at Doncaster in 1937. (British Railways)

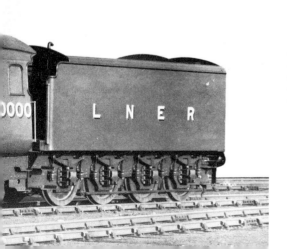

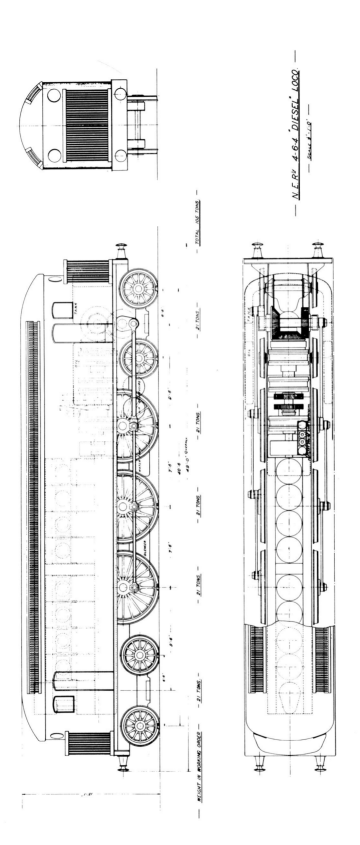

Drawing of proposed NER diesel locomotive.

Sir Vincent Raven favoured electrification but someone on the North Eastern must have had thoughts on dieselisation, as this drawing indicates. Nothing is known about this proposal and nothing has been located in NER records. It may have been a draughtsman's idea of things to come — or was it actually a serious proposal? The date, probably 1920-2.

Another proposal was for a six-coupled electric shunting locomotive, with a single electric motor mounted with the armature vertical, and a bevel drive to the centre axle. An experimental unit was built using the tender underframe off Class J 4-2-2 No 1525 withdrawn from Hull in August 1919. This unit was tried experimentally on the North Tyneside electric lines but it is odd that no exterior photograph of this engine has turned up, particularly when North Road Works photographed every new type of locomotive. However, an interior view has materialised and this shows the vertically mounted motor and the banks of resistances.

A drawing recently unearthed at the National Railway Museum shows that in 1910 there was a proposal for a three-cylinder version of the R1 4-4-0 of 1908, with 17in x 26in cylinders in place of the 19in x 26in cylinders on the two-cylinder engine. Raven actually asked permission to build 12 engines of this type and this was approved, but at some stage it was decided to increase the order to 20 and to change the wheel arrangement to 4-4-2. Consequently these appeared as the 10 class Z (saturated) and 10 class Z1 (superheated) Atlantics from the North British Locomotive Company in 1911.

12 LIGHT RAILWAYS ETC

The territory covered by the North Eastern Railway was, on the whole, so well served by the company's branch lines that there was little need for light railways to fill in the gaps. The main line between York and Darlington took the most direct course and missed the market town of Easingwold. Eventually an independent line was built from Easingwold to join the main line at Alne, 11 miles north of York, and from July 1891 to November 1948 a passenger and freight service was operated. After the withdrawal of the passenger service

the line continued to carry freight traffic until December 1957.

In Northumberland a similar line left the main line at Chathill to reach the small port of Seahouses and this service operated from December 1898 to October 1951. Each company received a large amount of help from its big neighbour and hired locomotives from the main line company when necessary.

A third line, the Cawood, Wistow & Selby Light Railway, opened in 1897 and commenced to carry passengers in February 1898. It was taken over by the North Eastern in 1900 and the passenger service continued to operate until 1 January 1930; the freight service, however, continued for many years and it was not withdrawn until May 1960.

Another standard gauge line was the Derwent Valley Light Railway which ran from its own terminus in York to a platform adjacent to the North Eastern at Cliff Common, on the Selby-Market Weighton line. The line opened in July 1913, and although the passenger service was withdrawn in 1926 the freight service continues to operate, although over only a small section of the original line between Layerthorpe (York) and Dunnington. The Derwent Valley Railway, the Light has been dropped from the title, pays an annual dividend, although it must be admitted that the profits to make this possible come from anything but the traffic receipts! However, in 1977 the DVR returned to the passenger business and started to operate a once-a-day seasonal service between Layerthorpe and Dunnington, hiring for the purpose a former BR J72 0-6-0T engine named Joem then owned privately; for the 1978 season the company purchased this locomotive. It is unfortunate that the daily train cannot operate to and from York BR station, where there is plenty of platform capacity available in the former Hull and Scarborough bays at the north end of the station.

The Nidd Valley Light Railway was built to serve Bradford Corporation reservoirs at the head of Nidderdale, but the section between Pateley Bridge and Loftus was opened as a public railway in 1907; although it closed to passengers from 1 January 1930 reservoir materials continued to be handled until 1936.

The narrow gauge Sand Hutton Light Railway was the pet project of Sir Robert Walker of Sand Hutton Hall and it started life as a 15in gauge pleasure line in 1912. Following World War I, with a quantity of surplus material available, it was decided to convert it into an 18in light railway and this was opened to passenger traffic on 4 October 1924. Unfortunately Sir Robert Walker died in February 1930 (at the age of 39) and the railway was closed five months later, on 7 July 1930.

A number of colliery systems in County Durham and Northumberland operated passenger services for their employees, the largest being that at Ashington, which continued in operation until 1966. The South Shields, Marsden & Whitburn system between Westoe Lane station in South Shields and Whitburn Colliery was basically a line for carrying pit employees but it was available to the public until it closed in November 1953 after being operated for almost seven years by the National Coal Board.

A view of the Sand Hutton Light Railway in its 18in days, with No 12 (built by the Hunslet Engine Company in 1917). The saloon coach was specially built for the SHLR and now, after many years of rotting away as a cricket pavilion, it has been restored and can be found in use on the Lincolnshire Coast Light Railway.

NORTH SUNDERLAND RAILWAY.

TIME TABLE

From 14th SEPTEMBER, 1931, to 30th APRIL, 1932.

		A.M.	A.M.	P.M.	P.M.	P.M.		
SEAHOUSES	dep.	*7 33	9 20	1 10	4 10	6 30		
CHATHILL	arr.	7 48	9 35	1 25	4 25	6 45		
		A.M.	A.M.	P.M.	P.M.	P.M.		
CHATHILL	dep.	*8 12	10 48	†2 0	†5 42	†6 55		
SEAHOUSES	arr.	8 27	11 3	2 15	5 57	7 10		

* Third Class (Parliamentary) Train.

† The 9.20 a.m., 12.22, 4.0 and 5.38 p.m. Express Trains from Newcastle stop at Chathill, connections arrive at Seahouses at 11.3 a.m., 2.15, 5.57 and 7.10 p.m.

THROUGH SERVICE.

In connection with L.N.E.R.

			A.M.	A.M.	P.M.	P.M.	E
Seahouses	-	- dep	7 33	9 20	1 10	4 10	6 30
Chathill -	-	- arr.	7 48	9 35	1 25	4 25	6 45
Alnmouth	-	- ,,	8 32	10 3	2 19	5 22	9 57
Alnwick	-	- ,,	8 54	10 27	2 43	5 37	10 15
Morpeth	-	- ,,	9 15	10 29	3 20	6 7	10 27
Newcastle	-	- ,,	9 45	10 56	3 50	6 39	11 2
Belford -	-	- ,,	8 18	10 41	1 46	5 28	7 2
Berwick	-	- ,,	9 0	11 7	2 6	5 50	7 22
				P.M.			
Edinburgh	-	- ,,		12 42	3 25	8 26	8 42

			A.M.	A.M.	A.M.	P.M.	P.M.
Edinburgh	-	- dep.		7 40	10 25	2 35	
					P.M.		
Berwick	-	- ,,	7 23	9 10	1 13	4 54	
Belford -	-	- ,,	7 56	9 33	1 46	5 27	
Newcastle	-	- ,,	6 12	9 20	12 22	4 0	5 38
Morpeth	-	- ,,	6 56	9 49	12 52	4 28	6 9
Alnwick	-	- ,,	7 20	9 55	1 5	4 48	6 22
Alnmouth	-	- ,,	7 33	10 19	1 28	5 9	6 35
Chathill	-	- ,,	8 12	10 48	2 0	5 42	6 55
Seahouses	-	- arr.	8 27	11 3	2 15	5 57	7 10

E—L.N.E.R train from Berwick calls at Chathill at 9.42 p.m. when required.

Fares.

	SINGLE.			RETURN.		
	1st Class.	2nd Class.	3rd Class. Parliamentary.	1st Class.	2nd Class.	3rd Class Parliamentary.
	s. d.	s. d.	s. d.	s. d.	s. d.	s. d.
Seahouses to Chathill -	1 2	0 11	0 9	2 4	1 10	1 6

Through Tickets

From Seahouses to :—	Experimental Fares		SINGLE.		RETURN.	
	3rd Class SINGLE.	3rd Class RETURN.	1st Class.	2nd Class to Chathill, 3rd beyond.	1st Class.	2nd Class to Chathill, 3rd beyond.
	s. d.	s. d.	s. d.	s. d.	s. d.	s. d.
Alnmouth - -	2 2	3 10	3 7	2 5	7 2	4 10
Alnwick - -	2 3	3 10	4 3	2 9	8 6	5 6
Belford - -			2 5	1 8	4 10	3 4
Berwick - -	•3 7		5 7	3 7	11 2	7 2
Heaton - -			10 6	6 6	21 0	13 0
Newcastle - -	•6 9		10 11	6 9	21 10	13 6
Tweedmouth -			5 4	3 5	10 8	6 10
Monkseaton (via Hartley)			10 1	6 3	20 2	12 6
Monkseaton (via Heaton)			12 2	7 6	24 4	15 0
Wallsend (via Heaton)			10 11	6 9	21 10	13 6
Tyne Dock and South Shields -			13 1	8 1	26 2	16 2

* Cheap tickets Thursdays and Saturdays, single fare for double journey.

PERIODICAL OR SEASON TICKETS.

SEAHOUSES TO CHATHILL.

12 MONTHS.		6 MONTHS.		3 MONTHS.		2 MONTHS.		1 MONTH.		14 DAYS.	
1st Class.	2nd Class.	1st Class.	2nd Class.	1st Class.	2nd Class.	1st Class.	2nd Class.	1st Class.	2nd Class.	1st Class.	2nd Class.
£ s. d.	£ s. d.	£ s. d.	£ s. d.	£ s. d.	£ s. d.	£ s. d.	£ s. d.	£ s. d.	£ s. d.	£ s. d.	£ s. d.
11 12 6	7 14 6	6 7 6	4 5 6	3 9 9	2 6 6	2 10 3	1 13 9	1 11 6	1 1 0	1 0 3	0 13 6

Periodical Tickets are issued at half-price to children under 15 years of age, and also to scholars, students, and apprentices learning a profession or trade, and not in receipt of salary, up to 18 years of age, on production by them of a Certificate from the Master of the School, the Principal of the College, or their Employer, as the case may be. A deposit of 5s. is required in respect of Periodical Tickets taken for a period of less than 3 months, such deposit will be returned to the Ticket Holder provided the ticket be given up on expiry.

The issuing of Tickets to Passengers to places off this Company's line is an arrangement made for the greater convenience of the public; but the Company will not be held responsible for the non-arrival of this Company's own trains in time for any nominally corresponding train on the London & North Eastern Company's line, nor for any delay, detention, or other loss or injury whatsoever which may arise therefrom, or for the acts or defaults of other parties, nor for the correctness of the times over the London & North Eastern Company's line.

PARCELS sent by Passenger Trains are received by the Company to be carried only on the same conditions relative to the times of the trains as stated in the notice above given.

N.B.—The hours or times stated in these Tables are appointed as those at which it is intended, as far as circumstances will permit, the Passenger Trains should depart from and arrive at Seahouses and Chathill respectively, but their departure or arrival at the times stated is not guaranteed, nor will the Company, under any circumstances, be held responsible for delay or detention, however occasioned, or any consequences arising therefrom.

61, Westgate Road, Newcastle-on-Tyne,
14th September, 1931.

RICHARD SMITH, Secretary.

JOHN BELL & CO., Printers, Railway Lane, Pilgrim Street, Newcastle.

Timetable for the North Sunderland Railway from 14 September 1931.

The Cawood, Wistow & Selby Light Railway on its last day of operation, 27 April 1960, with the Selby pilot D2063 at Wistow.

The advent of the National Railway Museum has brought in its wake an upsurge in railway interest and the Derwent Valley Railway now runs a daily passenger train from Layerthorpe to Dunnington and back, hauled by ex-British Rail J72 69023, now named Joem. This is the inaugural train on 4 May 1977, awaiting the Lord Mayor of York. At the time the locomotive was on hire to the DVR but it has since been purchased by the company.

The post-war period has seen many special trains for enthusiasts run over lines which had not seen a passenger train for many years. It did not matter if the decaying track would not take modern bogie coaches, open wagons would do! Fortunately on this day in June 1957 the weather was fine and the participants on this RCTS tour were quite happy to ride in the wagons from Alne to Easingwold and back. This is J71 68246 at Alne, with the tail end of the train in the short bay platform on the up side of the East Coast main line.

13 A COUPLE OF ODDITIES

More in the North West than in the North East, but North Eastern engines working the Wensleydale branch from Northallerton used this stockaded turntable at Garsdale (formerly Hawes Junction) in Midland Railway territory. (J W Armstrong)

An oddity on the Catterick Camp Military Railway was this line through a roundabout! (D Hardy)

A feature of railway operation in the North East, particularly in County Durham, was the rope worked incline, either self-acting or using a winding engine. The former could be used where the loaded wagons were descending the incline, but a winding engine had to be used where the loaded wagons were ascending the incline. Some inclines fell into disuse a century or more ago, such as the Etherley North incline on the Stockton & Darlington line of 1825. The chimney of the winding engine boiler can be seen through the arch of the bridge, which is still there, now filled in.

14 INCLINES

Some inclines lasted until well into British Railways' days, such as this self-acting incline at Lobley Hill, situated on the outskirts of Gateshead on the historic Tanfield wagonway, which pre-dated the Stockton & Darlington Railway. This typical view shows a loaded set of wagons, with bankrider, about to start its descent. (J W Armstrong)

Locomotive headboards were often used in the North East on special trains; here K3 2-6-0 46 passes Hartley bound for York, where the mainly juvenile passengers were to tour Rowntree's chocolate works, hence the headboard carrying the company's publicity gimmick of the period namely Mr York of York, Yorks.

15 LOCOMOTIVE HEADBOARDS

Excursions to Leeds were promoted by Lewis's store in the city and this engine worked a train which ran in January 1935; it is B16 2368, seen here at Neville Hill shed.

A special train for the employees of Bison Floors approaching Scarborough in 1959 when numerous NER signal gantries were still in use. These, together with Washbeck signalbox (on right) have now disappeared.

In Scarborough Central station and another employees' special has unloaded its passengers and awaits departure for the carriage sidings. This was in 1966 when diesel locomotives were supplanting steam engines!

THE NORTH EASTERN RAILWAY.

General Manager's Office,

CIRCULAR.

YORK, 17th March, 1874.

To Station Masters, Goods Agents, &c.

On the 1st April next the names of the undermentioned Stations on this railway will be altered, as follows : —

Sherburn (Y. N. & B.) to Sherburn Colliery.

Sherburn (D. & S.) to Sherburn House.

Sherburn (York and Scarbro') to Wykeham.

H. TENNANT.

GENERAL MANAGER.

An 1874 notice regarding the renaming of three NER stations all confusingly named Sherburn. A fourth Sherburn, on the York-Normanton line, was allowed to remain until it became Sherburn-in-Elmet in 1903. Wykeham was renamed Weaverthorpe in 1882 when a Wykeham station was provided on the new Seamer-Pickering line.

Railway companies often had to pay for water supplied to their engines by another company and the driver had to hand over a ticket so that the

---

NORTH EASTERN RAILWAY.

General Manager's Office,
York, July 28th, 1890.

CIRCULAR No. $\frac{437}{1890}$.

PRE-VICTORIAN GOLD COIN.

Station Masters and Goods Agents, Collectors, Booking Clerks, and others receiving money from the public on behalf of the Company are hereby instructed that Sovereigns and Half-Sovereigns bearing date earlier than the commencement of the reign of Queen Victoria must not in future be accepted in payment, as they are not now generally of full value, and have therefore been called in by the Authorities of the Mint.

H. TENNANT.

General Manager.

Queen Victoria ascended the throne in 1837, 53 years before the issue of this notice regarding sovereigns and half-sovereigns.

16 A QUARTET OF EPHEMERA

appropriate charge could be raised. A less common charge was for the use of another company's turntable.

LNER 7801/10/38 20,000   LR 7553

L.N.E.R. (_____Area)

Deliver to Driver_____

ENGINE No._____

Station_____

ONE_____ **of WATER**

Taken at_____

LOCOMOTIVE RUNNING SUPERINTENDENT.

Date_____

LNER 1692/2/33 10,000   L.R. 7554

L.N.E.R. (_____Area)

Please allow Driver_____

Station_____

TO TURN

ENGINE No._____

At_____Station.

LOCOMOTIVE RUNNING SUPERINTENDENT.

Date_____